31 Prayers & Reflec

Women's PRAYER Journal

By Josie Benjamin

This journal belongs to:

ISBN Paperback: 978-1-916691-92-6

ISBN Hardback: 978-1-916691-93-3

A Note from the Author

Hey Sis,

I created this journal to help you slow down and spend time with God in a personal way. Each page is designed to guide your heart into prayer, reflection, and honest conversation with Him. You will find scriptures to meditate on, prayers to inspire you, declarations to speak over your life, and space to write what is on your heart.

Take your time with every theme. Read the verses slowly, pray the prayers out loud, and write your thoughts and reflections freely. There is no right or wrong way to use it. This is your space to be open with God.

As you journey through these pages, may you learn to pray with purpose, trust with peace, and believe with audacious faith. Remember, God hears every word and holds every detail of your life with love and care.

With love,
Josie Benjamin

www.JosieBenjamin.org

Gratitude & Thanksgiving

Psalm 100:4–5

Enter into His gates with thanksgiving,
And into His courts with praise.
Be thankful to Him, and bless His name.
For the Lord is good; His mercy is everlasting, and His truth endures to all generations.

Declaration:

I choose gratitude and praise, trusting in God's enduring love and faithfulness.

Prayer:

Lord, I come with thanks and praise, embracing Your goodness. Let my heart overflow with gratitude as I trust in Your enduring love and promises.

My Prayer Today

- What blessings am I most grateful for in this season of my life?
- How can I express gratitude to God more intentionally each day?
- What happens to my perspective when I choose thankfulness over complaint?

Psalm 69:30

I will praise the name of God with a song,
And will magnify Him with thanksgiving.

My Reflections

Confidence

Psalm 27:1

The Lord is my light and my salvation;
Whom shall I fear?
The Lord is the strength of my life;
Of whom shall I be afraid?

Declaration:

I declare that God is my light and salvation. In Him, I find refuge and strength. Fear has no place in His presence.

Prayer:

Lord, You are my light and salvation. Strengthen and uphold me, and remove every trace of fear. Help me to walk in confidence in Your presence.

My Prayer Today

- Where do I need to trust God more deeply instead of relying on myself?
- How has fear held me back from walking boldly in faith?
- What truth about God's strength can I remind myself of when I feel afraid?

Isaiah 41:10

Fear not, for I am with you;
Be not dismayed, for I am your God.

My Reflections

Inner Beauty & Self-worth

1 Samuel 16:7

For the Lord does not see as man sees; for man looks at the outward appearance, but the Lord looks at the heart.

Declaration:

I seek God's heart and value what He values above all else.

Prayer:

Lord, You see my heart. Help me to value what You value and to find beauty in Your wisdom and virtue.

My Prayer Today

- How do I define beauty through God's eyes rather than the world's?
- What qualities in my character reflect God's heart?
- How can I remind myself of my worth when I feel overlooked or insecure?

Proverbs 31:30

Charm is deceitful and beauty is passing,
But a woman who fears the Lord, she shall be praised.

My Reflections

Identity

1 Peter 2:9

You are a chosen generation, a royal priesthood, a holy nation, His own special people, that you may proclaim the praises of Him who called you out of darkness into His marvellous light.

Declaration:

I embrace my identity as God's chosen one, called to proclaim His praises.

Prayer:

Lord, help me embrace my identity as Your chosen child. May my life declare Your praises and reflect Your light.

My Prayer Today

- What does it mean to live as one who has been chosen by God?
- How does knowing I am fearfully and wonderfully made affect how I see myself?
- What lies about my identity do I need to surrender to God's truth?

Psalm 139:14

I will praise You, for I am fearfully and wonderfully made;
Marvellous are Your works,
and that my soul knows very well.

My Reflections

Purpose

Proverbs 19:21

There are many plans in a man's heart, Nevertheless the Lord's counsel; that will stand.

Declaration:

I surrender my plans to God and trust His purpose to prevail in my life.

Prayer:

Lord, I surrender my plans to You. May Your purpose prevail in my life, and grant me wisdom to walk in the works You have prepared.

My Prayer Today

- What dreams or plans do I need to surrender to God's will?
- How do I recognise the difference between my plans and His purpose?
- What steps can I take today to walk in the path He has prepared for me?

Ephesians 2:10

For we are His workmanship, created in Christ Jesus for good works, which God prepared beforehand that we should walk in them.

My Reflections

Strength & Resilience

Philippians 4:13
I can do all things through Christ who strengthens me.

Declaration:
I do all things through Christ who strengthens me and face challenges with perseverance and courage.

Prayer:

Lord, in Your strength I can do all things. Renew my spirit and give me courage to face challenges with faith.

My Prayer Today

- When have I seen God's strength carry me through weakness?
- What current challenge is building spiritual endurance in me?
- How can I renew my strength daily in His presence?

Isaiah 40:31

But those who wait on the Lord shall renew their strength; They shall mount up with wings like eagles, They shall run and not be weary, They shall walk and not faint.

My Reflections

Relationships

Ecclesiastes 4:9–10

Two are better than one,
Because they have a good reward for their labour. For if they fall, one will lift up his companion. But woe to him who is alone when he falls, For he has no one to help him up.

Declaration:

I value the gift of companionship and love others as Christ loved the church.

Prayer:

Lord, thank You for the gift of companionship. Teach me to love sacrificially and to value the people You place in my life.

My Prayer Today

- How can I be more supportive and present in my relationships?
- What relationships need healing or forgiveness right now?
- How can I reflect Christ's love more clearly to those around me?

Ephesians 5:25

Husbands, love your wives, just as Christ also loved the church and gave Himself for her.

My Reflections

Healing

Psalm 147:3

He heals the broken-hearted
And binds up their wounds.

Declaration:

I receive God's healing as He binds up my wounds with His love and grace.

Prayer:

Lord, heal the brokenness within me and bind up my wounds with Your love and grace.

My Prayer Today

- What areas of my heart still need healing and restoration?
- How has God already begun to heal parts of my life?
- What truth about His love brings me comfort in moments of pain?

Matthew 9:35

Then Jesus went about all the cities and villages, teaching in their synagogues, preaching the gospel of the kingdom, and healing every sickness and every disease among the people.

My Reflections

Restoration

Joel 2:25–26

So I will restore to you the years that the swarming locust has eaten.
You shall eat in plenty and be satisfied,
And praise the name of the Lord your God,
Who has dealt wondrously with you.

Declaration:

I trust in God's promise of restoration and rejoice in His faithfulness.

Prayer:

Lord, thank You for restoring what has been lost. Fill my heart with the joy of Your salvation and renew a steadfast spirit within me.

My Prayer Today

- What losses or disappointments do I need to trust God to restore?
- How can I stay hopeful while waiting for His restoration?
- What does "the joy of His salvation" look like in my life right now?

Psalm 51:12

Restore to me the joy of Your salvation,
And uphold me by Your generous Spirit.

My Reflections

Fear & Anxiety

1 Peter 5:7

Casting all your care upon Him, for He cares for you.

Declaration:

I cast all my cares on God and receive His peace that guards my heart and mind.

Prayer:

Lord, I cast all my anxieties upon You. Help me to trust Your love and rest in Your peace.

My Prayer Today

- What fears have I been holding onto instead of giving to God?
- How can I practise peace in moments of stress or uncertainty?
- What helps me remember that God's care is greater than my worry?

Philippians 4:6

Be anxious for nothing, but in everything by prayer and supplication, with thanksgiving, let your requests be made known to God..

My Reflections

Joy & Contentment

Philippians 4:11–12

I have learned in whatever state I am, to be content. I know how to be abased, and I know how to abound. Everywhere and in all things I have learned both to be full and to be hungry, both to abound and to suffer need.

Declaration:

I find contentment in every circumstance and walk in the fullness of joy found in God's presence.

Prayer:

Lord, teach me contentment in every circumstance. Let my joy be rooted in Your presence, where there is fullness of life.

My Prayer Today

- What does true contentment look like in my daily life?
- How can I nurture joy even when circumstances are difficult?
- What simple things has God given me that bring delight and peace?

Psalm 16:11

You will show me the path of life;
In Your presence is fullness of joy;
At Your right hand are pleasures forevermore.

My Reflections

Trust

Proverbs 3:5–6

Trust in the Lord with all your heart,
And lean not on your own understanding;
In all your ways acknowledge Him,
And He shall direct your paths.

Declaration:

I trust in the Lord and acknowledge Him in all my ways, and He directs my path.

Prayer:

Lord, I trust You with all my heart. Direct my paths and help me to lean not on my own understanding.

My Prayer Today

- Where am I still leaning on my own understanding instead of trusting God?
- What experiences have strengthened my trust in His guidance?
- How can I remind myself of His faithfulness when I feel unsure?

Psalm 56:3–4

Whenever I am afraid, I will trust in You.
In God I have put my trust; I will not fear.
What can flesh do to me?

My Reflections

Surrender

James 4:7
Therefore submit to God. Resist the devil and he will flee from you.

Declaration:
I submit myself to God and resist the devil. I offer my life as a living sacrifice, pleasing to Him.

Prayer:

Lord, I surrender completely to You. Help me to resist temptation and walk in obedience. May my life be a living sacrifice that brings You glory.

My Prayer Today

- What areas of my life do I still need to fully surrender to God?
- What does submission to His will look like in this season?
- How can I make surrender part of my daily walk?

Romans 12:1

I beseech you therefore, brethren, by the mercies of God, that you present your bodies a living sacrifice, holy, acceptable to God, which is your reasonable service.

My Reflections

Business

Proverbs 10:22

The blessing of the Lord makes one rich,
And He adds no sorrow with it.

Declaration:

I walk in God's blessing and wisdom. His favour prospers the work of my hands and adds no sorrow with it.

Prayer:

Lord, thank You for blessing the work of my hands. Help me to steward every opportunity with wisdom and integrity, and may my efforts bring You glory.

My Prayer Today

- How can I honour God through the way I work or run my business?
- What areas of my work need more prayer and wisdom?
- How can I ensure that success never replaces faithfulness?

Psalm 128:1–2

Blessed is every one who fears the Lord,
Who walks in His ways. When you eat the labour of your hands, You shall be happy, and it shall be well with you.

My Reflections

Faith

Hebrews 11:1

Now faith is the substance of things hoped for, the evidence of things not seen.

Declaration:

I have faith in things hoped for and evidence of things not seen. I trust in God's faithfulness.

Prayer:

Lord, strengthen my faith to believe even when I cannot see. Help me to trust in Your promises and walk boldly in confidence.

My Prayer Today

- What does it mean to truly live by faith and not by sight?
- How has God proven Himself faithful to me in the past?
- What "mountain" do I need to believe God can move right now?

Matthew 17:20

If you have faith as a mustard seed, you will say to this mountain, “Move from here to there,” and it will move; and nothing will be impossible for you.

My Reflections

Hope

Jeremiah 29:11

For I know the thoughts that I think toward you, says the Lord, thoughts of peace and not of evil, to give you a future and a hope.

Declaration:

I am filled with joy and peace as I trust in God. My hope abounds through the power of the Holy Spirit.

Prayer:

Lord, fill me with hope that never fades. Help me to trust Your plans for my life and find peace in Your promises.

My Prayer Today

- What promise from God fills me with hope for the future?
- How can I keep hope alive during waiting seasons?
- What habits strengthen my hope instead of draining it?

Romans 15:13

Now may the God of hope fill you with all joy and peace in believing, that you may abound in hope by the power of the Holy Spirit.

My Reflections

Royalty

Isaiah 62:3

You shall be a crown of glory in the hand of the Lord, and a royal diadem in the hand of your God.

Declaration:

I am a crown of glory in the hand of the Lord and a royal diadem in the hand of my God, set apart as His beloved daughter.

Prayer:

Lord, I embrace my royal identity in You. Help me to walk with dignity, humility, and purpose as Your chosen child.

My Prayer Today

- What does it mean for me to live as God's royal child?
- How can I carry myself with dignity and humility at the same time?
- What "royal responsibilities" come with being chosen by God?

Galatians 3:29

And if you are Christ's, then you are Abraham's seed, and heirs according to the promise.

My Reflections

Longevity

Psalm 91:16

With long life I will satisfy him,
And show him My salvation.

Declaration:

I walk in the promise of long life, wisdom, and honour under God's divine protection.

Prayer:

Lord, thank You for the promise of long life and divine protection. Help me to walk in wisdom, honour, and obedience to Your word.

My Prayer Today

- What does a long, fruitful life look like to me in God's eyes?
- How can I steward my body, mind, and spirit wisely each day?
- What promises of protection bring me peace and confidence?

Proverbs 3:16
Length of days is in her right hand,
In her left hand riches and honour.

My Reflections

Singleness

Isaiah 54:5

For your Maker is your husband,
The Lord of hosts is His name;
And your Redeemer is the Holy One of Israel; He is called the God of the whole earth.

Declaration:

I take courage in God's constant presence and trust Him to fulfil every desire according to His will.

Prayer:

Lord, thank You that I am never alone. You are my companion and strength. Help me to delight in You and trust Your perfect timing for every area of my life.

My Prayer Today

- How can I enjoy this season of singleness as a time of growth and intimacy with God?
- What promises remind me that God's timing is perfect?
- How can I prepare my heart for future seasons without losing hope?

Psalm 37:4

Delight yourself also in the Lord,
And He shall give you the desires of your heart.

My Reflections

Confession & Repentance

James 5:16

Confess your trespasses to one another, and pray for one another, that you may be healed. The effective, fervent prayer of a righteous man avails much.

Declaration:

I confess my sins to God, who is faithful and just to forgive and cleanse me from all unrighteousness.

Prayer:

Lord, I confess my sins before You. Cleanse my heart and restore me to right standing with You.

My Prayer Today

- What do I need to confess and release to walk in freedom?
- How has forgiveness from God changed my life?
- How can I live daily with a soft, repentant heart before Him?

1 John 1:9

If we confess our sins, He is faithful and just to forgive us our sins and to cleanse us from all unrighteousness.

My Reflections

Loneliness

Deuteronomy 31:8

And the Lord, He is the One who goes before you. He will be with you, He will not leave you nor forsake you; do not fear nor be dismayed.

Declaration:

I am never alone. God is with me through every storm, and His strength upholds me.

Prayer:

Lord, thank You that You are with me in every season. When I feel alone, remind me that Your presence surrounds and sustains me.

My Prayer Today

- What truths remind me that I am never alone?
- How can I recognise God's presence even in quiet or empty moments?
- What helps me stay connected to others when I feel isolated?

Isaiah 43:2

When you pass through the waters, I will be with you;
And through the rivers, they shall not overflow you.
When you walk through the fire, you shall not be burned...

My Reflections

Heartbreak

Psalm 34:18

The Lord is near to those who have a broken heart,
And saves such as have a contrite spirit.

Declaration:

God is near to me and heals my broken heart. His strength upholds me and His love makes me whole.

Prayer:

Lord, heal my broken heart and draw near in my pain. Let Your love restore and comfort me in every hidden place.

My Prayer Today

- What pain do I need to hand over to God for healing?
- How has heartbreak shaped my understanding of His love?
- What can I thank Him for, even in my broken places?

Isaiah 41:10

Fear not, for I am with you; Be not dismayed, for I am your God. I will strengthen you, Yes, I will help you, I will uphold you with My righteous right hand.

My Reflections

Provision

Philippians 4:19

And my God shall supply all your need according to His riches in glory by Christ Jesus.

Declaration:

God supplies all my needs. He is my shepherd, and I lack nothing.

Prayer:

Lord, thank You for being my shepherd and provider. I trust You to meet every need according to Your riches and grace.

My Prayer Today

- Where have I seen God's provision in the past?
- How can I grow in faith to depend on His supply, not my own?
- What does trusting Him with my resources look like today?

Psalm 23:1

The Lord is my shepherd;
I shall not want.

My Reflections

Forgiveness

Ephesians 4:32

And be kind to one another, tender-hearted, forgiving one another, even as God in Christ forgave you.

Declaration:

I choose kindness and forgiveness, extending grace as God has given it to me.

Prayer:

Lord, help me to forgive others as You have forgiven me. Heal my heart from bitterness and fill me with compassion and grace.

My Prayer Today

- Who do I need to forgive to walk in full freedom?
- How has unforgiveness affected my peace and joy?
- How can I reflect God's grace to others through forgiveness?

Colossians 3:13

Bearing with one another, and forgiving one another, if anyone has a complaint against another; even as Christ forgave you, so you also must do.

My Reflections

Peace

Philippians 4:6–7

Be anxious for nothing, but in everything by prayer and supplication, with thanksgiving, let your requests be made known to God;

and the peace of God, which surpasses all understanding, will guard your hearts and minds through Christ Jesus.

Declaration:

I receive God's peace. My heart is not troubled, and my mind is guarded by His presence.

Prayer:

Lord, fill my heart with Your peace that surpasses understanding. Let Your presence quiet every fear and bring calm to my soul.

My Prayer Today

- What steals my peace and how can I guard my heart against it?
- How can I create moments of quiet to hear God's voice?
- What truth about His peace do I need to meditate on today?

John 14:27

Peace I leave with you, My peace I give to you; not as the world gives do I give to you. Let not your heart be troubled, neither let it be afraid.

My Reflections

Obedience

Deuteronomy 28:1–2

Now it shall come to pass, if you diligently obey the voice of the Lord your God, to observe carefully all His commandments which I command you today, that the Lord your God will set you high above all nations of the earth. And all these blessings shall come upon you and overtake you, because you obey the voice of the Lord your God.

Declaration:

I walk in obedience to God's word and receive the blessings that come from honouring His voice.

Prayer:

Lord, help me to be not only a hearer but a doer of Your word. Give me a heart that delights in obedience.

My Prayer Today

- What is God asking me to do that requires faith and obedience?
- How can I respond more quickly when I sense His leading?
- What blessings have I experienced from obeying His word?

James 1:22

But be doers of the word, and not hearers only, deceiving yourselves.

My Reflections

Wisdom

Proverbs 2:6

For the Lord gives wisdom;
From His mouth come knowledge and understanding.

Declaration:

I am guided by the wisdom of God. His understanding leads my steps and brings clarity to every decision.

Prayer:

Lord, grant me divine wisdom and understanding. Teach me to make choices that honour You and guide me to walk in discernment and truth.

My Prayer Today

- Where in my life do I need greater wisdom right now?
- How can I develop the habit of seeking God before making decisions?
- What has God already taught me through past mistakes?

James 1:5

If any of you lacks wisdom, let him ask of God, who gives to all liberally and without reproach, and it will be given to him.

My Reflections

Patience

Romans 12:12
Rejoicing in hope, patient in tribulation, continuing steadfastly in prayer.

Declaration:
I walk in patience and perseverance, trusting God's perfect timing and remaining steadfast in hope.

Prayer:

Father, help me to wait on You with patience and peace. Remind me that Your timing is perfect and that every delay is preparation for greater blessing.

My Prayer Today

- What situation is testing my patience and trust in God's timing?
- How can I turn waiting into worship instead of frustration?
- What promises remind me that His delays are never denial?

Galatians 6:9

And let us not grow weary while doing good, for in due season we shall reap if we do not lose heart.

My Reflections

Humility

Philippians 2:3

Let nothing be done through selfish ambition or conceit, but in lowliness of mind let each esteem others better than himself.

Declaration:

I walk humbly before God, showing mercy and honouring others with a gentle and willing heart.

Prayer:

Lord, give me a humble heart. Remove pride and self-centredness, and teach me to serve with love and grace. May humility mark my walk with You.

My Prayer Today

- How can I practise humility in my daily interactions?
- What attitudes or habits might be rooted in pride?
- How can I better reflect Jesus' servant heart?

Micah 6:8

He has shown you, O man, what is good;
And what does the Lord require of you But to do justly,
to love mercy, And to walk humbly with your God?

My Reflections

Courage

Joshua 1:9

Have I not commanded you? Be strong and of good courage; do not be afraid, nor be dismayed, for the Lord your God is with you wherever you go.

Declaration:

I am strong and courageous. The Lord strengthens my heart and goes with me wherever I go.

Prayer:

God, fill me with courage to face every challenge without fear. Strengthen my heart and remind me that You are always with me.

My Prayer Today

- What fears am I facing that require courage to overcome?
- How can I remind myself daily that God is with me wherever I go?
- What step of faith can I take today to walk in boldness?

Psalm 31:24

Be of good courage, and He shall strengthen your heart,
All you who hope in the Lord.

My Reflections

Faithfulness

Lamentations 3:22–23

Through the Lord's mercies we are not consumed,
Because His compassions fail not.
They are new every morning;
Great is Your faithfulness.

Declaration:

God's faithfulness sustains me. I remain steadfast in love, obedience, and devotion to His purpose.

Prayer:

Lord, thank You for Your unfailing faithfulness. Help me to mirror that same faithfulness in my walk with You and in every relationship and assignment You entrust to me.

My Prayer Today

- In what areas of my life can I become more consistent and faithful?
- How has God's faithfulness inspired me to persevere?
- What does being faithful with "small things" look like today?

Proverbs 3:3–4

Let not mercy and truth forsake you; Bind them around your neck, Write them on the tablet of your heart, and so find favour and high esteem In the sight of God and man.

My Reflections

Prayer Requests and Answers

Prayer Request	Prayer Date	Date Answered

Prayer Requests and Answers

Prayer Request	Prayer Date	Date Answered

Notes

Notes

Notes

Notes

Notes

Printed in Dunstable, United Kingdom

73254363R00078